GW01184556

Bully boys

John and Marilyn Talbot

Illustrated by Mike Lacey

Nelson

Contents

Chapter I What's wrong?

'Are you coming out?' Kevin asked.

'No, I can't,' said Rocky.

'Why not?' said Kevin.

'I've got something to do,' said Rocky.

'What?' Kevin asked.

'Just something,' said Rocky.

'OK,' said Kevin, as he walked away.

'See you later then.'

'Right. See you later,' said Rocky, as he closed the front door.

But Kevin didn't see Rocky later.

Rocky hadn't been out with his friends for a long time.

Rocky said the same thing when Tony asked him to come out.

He could not come out because he had something to do.

'Are you OK?' Tony asked.

'Yes,' said Rocky.

But he didn't look OK, and he didn't sound OK.

Anyone could see that he didn't look at all happy.

Rocky wasn't going anywhere with anyone.

Not one of his friends saw him these days.

The only time he ever went out was to walk Max, his dog.

Then Rocky started to have days off school.
'What's wrong, Rocky? You can tell me,' said his Mum.
'I just don't feel very well,' said Rocky.
'Where does it hurt?' asked Mrs Rockwell. 'Is it
your head?'
She put her hand on Rocky's head.
'No,' said Rocky. 'I just don't feel well, all over.'
Mrs Rockwell looked at Rocky.
It was true. He didn't look very well.
'Right. I'll telephone the school,' she said.

'I'm afraid Rocky won't be coming to school today,'
said Mrs Rockwell. 'He's not feeling very well.'
'Oh, I'm sorry to hear that,' said Mrs Jones, the
Head Teacher. 'Is he very ill?'
'No,' said Mrs Rockwell. 'I'm not sure what's wrong.
Rocky just isn't feeling so good today.'
'Well, I hope he will be back at school soon,' said
Mrs Jones. 'We all miss Rocky when he isn't here,
and he has had a lot of days off this term.'
'I know,' said Mrs Rockwell. 'He should be
back tomorrow.'
'That's good,' said Mrs Jones. 'Thank you for
calling. Goodbye.'

'I've telephoned your Head Teacher,'
Mrs Rockwell told Rocky.
'What did she say?' asked Rocky.
'She said you had been having a lot of days
off school this term,' said his Mum, 'so it's back to
school tomorrow for you, my lad!'

The next day Rocky was back at school.
But he didn't play with any of his friends.
He just kept to himself.
'What's up with Rocky?' Ben asked.
'I don't know,' said Kevin. 'He's just no fun any more.'

'Something is wrong with Rocky,' said Tony.
'What?' Tessa asked.
'I don't know, but he's never been like this before,'
said Tony.
Everyone seemed to be thinking the same thing.
Something was wrong with Rocky. But what?

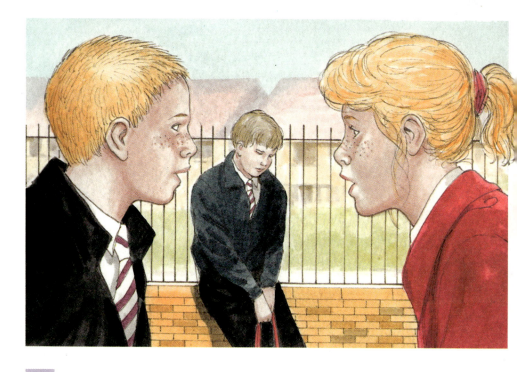

Chapter 2 Comic stuff

'I want you all to make your own comic,'
said Mr Belter.
'I want you to write it and draw the pictures,' he said,
'and I would like you to work in teams. Three people
in each team. So, without making too much noise, get
together with your team as I call out your names.'
Then Mr Belter called out the names of the
children in each team.

Mr Belter got to team five.
'Team five will be, Kevin Miller, Tessa Potts and Rocky Rockwell,' he said.
Kevin came over to Tessa and Rocky.
He was smiling.
'This is going to be great,' said Kevin.
'Why?' asked Tessa.
'Because I always wanted to make my own comic,'
he said. 'I have lots at home. I love to read them.'

When everyone was in their teams, Mr Belter told them that the very best comic would go into the school newspaper, 'The Waterloo News', next week.
Lots of hands went up.
One of them was Kevin's.
'Yes, Kevin?' said Mr Belter.
'Can we have a Super-hero in our comic?'
'Yes,' said Mr Belter, 'you can have a Super-hero. But it must be your own Super-hero. You must make it up.'
'Great,' said Kevin.

More hands went up.
This time it was Rocky.
'Yes, Rocky?' said Mr Belter.
'Can we have Super-villains too?' asked Rocky quietly.
'Yes, you can write about Super-villains. But again, they must be your own Super-villains,' said Mr Belter.

'Take a few minutes to talk about what you're going to do. Then you can start,' said Mr Belter.
'I have a good idea,' said Kevin, and he began to write something down.
'Do you have an idea?' Tessa asked Rocky.
'Yes,' said Rocky, 'I do have an idea.'
Slowly, Rocky began to speak, and when he did the others stopped what they were doing to listen.
Both Kevin and Tessa were surprised by Rocky's idea.
'It's brilliant!' said Kevin.

Soon they were coming up with their own ideas to help Rocky.
'We need a good name for the Super-villains,' said Rocky.
'How about the 'Mad Dogs'?' said Kevin.
'Great!' said Rocky.
'Now we need a name for the Super-hero,' said Rocky.
They all thought for a minute.
'What about T-shirt Man?' said Tessa.
They all thought this was really funny.
This was the first time Rocky had laughed in a long while.
Then Mr Belter came over.
'I'm pleased you're having so much fun doing your comic,' he said.

T-shirt Man

It was a quiet day for T-shirt Man.
He was out doing what
Super-heroes do.
He was looking for villains!
It's true, T-shirt Man didn't look
like a Super-hero. He did not look
like a Super-hero in his street
clothes.

1

Down the street a young boy
was out walking his dog by the
canal.

2

Suddenly some villains, who
went by the name of the
'Mad Dogs', jumped out on
him. The boy was frightened.

3

What do you want?

4

What do we want?

What have you got?

They laughed and made fun of him.
Then they stopped laughing.

5

Well then, we will keep your little dog ...
... while you go home and get some money for us.

6

No!

7

Yes!
Tell no-one, or your little dog
goes swimming with a weight!

The boy ran home as fast as
he could while the 'Mad
Dogs' played with his pet.

8

15

T-shirt Man heard the noise and quickly changed into his Super-hero clothes.
All he had to do was pull his T-shirt over his head, like they do in football when they get a goal. He had a hole for each eye so he could see. His Super-hero face was on the inside of his T-shirt!

He flew down the street.
He flew up onto the roof of a house.

11

10

They are always making trouble, but today trouble has come to them. Let's see if they like it!

He looked down on the 'Mad Dogs' having their fun.

12

16

Then he chased after the 'Mad Dogs'.

17

The 'Mad Dogs' ran into a shop.

Frozen Foods

Peas

18

When T-shirt Man followed they threw things at him. Tins! A bottle of drink!

19

Vegetables!
Bags of sweets! Bread.
Chocolate bars! Bananas!
They threw anything they could get their hands on!

SMASH!
CRASH!

20

T-shirt Man moved so fast that nothing hit him. But he hit them.

POW!

21

By Team 5.

Chapter 4 Walking the dog

Rocky was off school the next day.
The Head Teacher asked Mr Belter to come and
see her.
'I wanted to ask you about Rocky,' said Mrs Jones.
'How can I help?' said Mr Belter.
'Have you noticed anything wrong with Rocky?'
she asked.
'Yes, I have,' said Mr. Belter. 'Rocky is very quiet in
class these days. Usually he is a happy boy, and full
of fun. But now he doesn't talk much at all.'
'Why do you think that is?' asked Mrs Jones.
'I really don't know,' said Mr Belter.
'Well, keep an eye on him when he comes back,
would you?' said Mrs Jones.
Mr Belter said he would, and went out.

On the way back to his class
Mr Belter remembered that
Rocky had asked him
something yesterday.
He had asked him about
villains.
'Perhaps Rocky is in some
kind of trouble,' he thought.

Back in the classroom Mr Belter was trying to find
the best comic.
'They are all so good,' he thought.
'It's so difficult to say which one is best.'
Then Mr Belter read the comic from team five.
He laughed when he read about T-shirt Man.
But then he stopped laughing because he was
surprised at what he saw.
In team five there were Kevin, Tessa and Rocky.

Then Mr Belter called Tessa and Kevin over to him.
'I like your comic very much,' he said.
'Who thought of the idea?'
'We all did,' said Kevin.
'Yes, but Rocky thought of the idea first,' said Tessa.
'Do you think this could be true?' asked Mr Belter.
'Don't be silly, Mr Belter. T-shirt Man isn't real!'
Kevin laughed.
'I know that T-shirt Man isn't real,' said
Mr Belter quietly.
'What I mean is, do you think someone is getting at
Rocky, like the boy in the comic?'
Kevin and Tessa looked at each other.
'Someone could be,' said Tessa.
'Who knows?' said Kevin.

On the way home Kevin and Tessa talked together.
'Mr Belter may be right,' said Tessa.
'I know,' said Kevin, 'but if he's right, what can we
do about it?'
'We could ask Rocky,' said Tessa.
'He won't tell us, not if he's really frightened,'
said Kevin.
'Why not?' asked Tessa.
'Because if they find out that Rocky told us he
might be in a lot more trouble,' said Kevin.
Tessa was surprised.
'I see,' she said. 'But how do you know so
much about it, Kevin?'

Then Kevin spoke quietly.
'Because I was a bully once,' he said, 'so I know
how they think. I always picked on someone who
couldn't hit back. Someone small, who would do as
I told them.'
'But you're not a bully any more, are you?' said Tessa.
'No, not now. Not like I once was,' said Kevin.

When Tessa got home, her Dad made her some tea.
Then she had an idea and telephoned Kevin.
'I've thought of something,' Tessa said.
'What is it?' asked Kevin.
'Why don't we follow Rocky and see if anyone
gives him trouble?'
'We can't follow Rocky all the time,' said Kevin,
'that's stupid.'
'Not all the time,' said Tessa, 'only when he's
walking Max. Remember the comic!'
'Yes, you're right,' said Kevin. 'Let's start today!'
'OK,' said Tessa, 'see you later!'

'We don't want him to see us,' said Tessa.
So, as they followed Rocky and his dog, they kept a
full street between them.
All the time they hid behind cars and walls so
Rocky wouldn't see them.
They went out of Wellington Square, along
street after street.
Then Rocky turned down by the canal and past the
narrow-boat, the Mary Ann.
Sure enough, three boys were there, waiting for him.
Tessa and Kevin couldn't hear what they were saying.
But anyone could see Rocky was frightened of them.

'This is just like the comic,'
said Tessa.
'Yes, they are the
'Mad Dogs',' said Kevin.
'All we need now is
T-shirt Man,' said Tessa.
'Yes,' said Kevin, 'and I think
I know where to find him!'
Trying not to be seen, Kevin
ran over to the Mary Ann.

Tessa watched and waited.
'What's he doing?' she thought. 'Hurry up! Hurry up!'
Suddenly she saw T-shirt Man come out of the
narrow-boat!
Tessa couldn't believe her eyes.

By now the big boys were giving Rocky a hard time.
They shook him and pushed him.
'Hey! Leave that boy alone!' T-shirt Man shouted.
The boys all turned and looked.
They got a big surprise.
They saw a big man running towards them, with a
T-shirt over his head. He looked like a monster!
They turned and ran for their lives.
'If I see you around here again, you're in big trouble!'
T-shirt Man shouted after them.

When the bully boys were gone, T-shirt Man pulled back his T-shirt.
It was Jack.
'Jack always did like a good joke,' said Peg, as she came out of the narrow-boat.
Jack and Peg lived on the narrow-boat together.
'That's the best fun I've had in a long time!'
Jack laughed.
They all went inside the narrow-boat.
Jack made some tea for everyone.
Rocky told them all about the bully boys.
'Why didn't you tell someone?' asked Peg.
'I was too frightened,' said Rocky.
'You should always tell someone,' said Jack. 'Never let anyone bully you like that again.'
'I won't,' said Rocky, 'now that I've met the real T-shirt Man.'
Everyone laughed.

Chapter 5 Best comic

Back at school Rocky was his happy self once more.
Everyone was pleased to have him back again.
Mrs Jones called all of the school together in the Hall.
'Will Tessa Potts, Kevin Miller and Rocky Rockwell
come up to the front, please,' said Mrs Jones.
All three got up. They walked out in front of the other
children.

'Your comic is the best. It will go into our next school newspaper,' said Mrs Jones.

'It's both clever and funny,' she said, holding up their work.

She went on, 'It is about bully boys. But do they get away with it? No, because T-shirt Man comes to the rescue!'

Everyone in the Hall laughed.

As they were going out of the Hall, Kevin thought this was a good time to tell Mr Belter what had happened.
'You were right, Mr Belter, there is a real
T-shirt Man,' he said.
'Yes, well done Kevin. You've had your fun. Now move along,' said his teacher.
'But what I'm saying is true,' said Kevin.
'Come on, Kevin,' said Mr Belter. 'You're holding everyone up. Please move along.'
'Yes, Mr Belter,' said Kevin.

When the school newspaper came out, Kevin, Tessa and Rocky showed one to Jack and Peg on their narrow-boat.

'Those boys haven't given you any more trouble, have they?' Jack asked.

'No,' said Rocky, 'they haven't.'

'Yes,' said Peg, 'thanks to our Super-hero, T-shirt Man!'